EPHESIANS

WHOLENESS FOR A BROKEN WORLD

ANDREW T. &
PHYLLIS J.
LE PEAU

11 STUDIES
FOR INDIVIDUALS
OR GROUPS

Life
Builder
Study

INTER-VARSITY PRESS
36 Causton Street, London SW1P 4ST, England
Email: ivp@ivpbooks.com
Website: www.ivpbooks.com

Originally published in the United States of America in the LifeGuide® Bible Studies series in 1985 by InterVarsity Press, Downers Grove, Illinois
Second edition published in 2000
First published in Great Britain by Scripture Union in 2000
This edition published in Great Britain by Inter-Varsity Press 2019

British Library Cataloguing-in-Publication Data
A catalogue record for this book is available from the British Library.

ISBN: 978–1–78359–836–6

Printed in Great Britain by Ashford Colour Press Ltd, Gosport, Hampshire

Contents

Getting the Most
Out of *Ephesians*

Let's face it. Most of us are problem-centered. How will I get all my work done on time? What can I do to be a better witness? Why isn't my ministry more effective?

Solving all these problems is good. But so often we lack a broader perspective. We put Band-Aids over gaping wounds instead of looking for long-term solutions. We lack vision so we fail to ask why we are involved in these activities at all.

We have enjoyed going back again and again to Paul's letter to the Ephesians because it communicates the Christian vision more powerfully and succinctly than any of his other letters. Most of Paul's other letters are directed to the particular problems of a given church. For example, he wrote to the Galatians about the threat of legalism. He addressed a variety of problems at the church at Corinth. But his letter to the Ephesians is blissfully free from turmoil.

Some believe the letter has this quality because it was not written solely for the church at Ephesus. Rather it was probably a circular letter sent to the Christian communities of Asia and other provinces, especially where Paul was not personally known. While most of his letters are full of personal greetings, no individuals are mentioned here or greeted by name. In fact the oldest and best manuscripts even lack the words *in Ephesus* (1:1). They are addressed generally "to the saints who are also faithful in Christ Jesus." But at an early date the letter became associated with the Ephesian church, so most later manuscripts have "to the saints in Ephesus, the faithful in Christ Jesus."

Ultimately, however, this letter is written to us, whoever the original readers were. It enables us to see the full sweep of God's program from before creation to the ultimate union of everyone and everything in Jesus Christ. It puts our problems and our entire lives in the context of eternity.

This guide offers you the opportunity to capture God's vision for all of history by studying Ephesians. It comes in the form of eleven studies for individuals or groups. Each study covers about half a chapter. But they are not isolated, independent discussions but rather build on each other.

May Ephesians expand your vision of what God is doing in history and give you wholeness in this broken world.

Suggestions for Individual Study

1. As you begin each study, pray that God will speak to you through his Word.

2. Read the introduction to the study and respond to the personal reflection question or exercise. This is designed to help you focus on God and on the theme of the study.

3. Each study deals with a particular passage—so that you can delve into the author's meaning in that context. Read and reread the passage to be studied. If you are studying a book, it will be helpful to read through the entire book prior to the first study. The questions are written using the language of the New International Version, so you may wish to use that version of the Bible. The New Revised Standard Version is also recommended.

4. This is an inductive Bible study, designed to help you discover for yourself what Scripture is saying. The study includes three types of questions. *Observation* questions ask about the basic facts: who, what, when, where and how. *Interpretation* questions delve into the meaning of the passage. *Application* questions help you discover the implications of the text for growing in Christ. These three keys unlock the treasures of Scripture.

Write your answers to the questions in the spaces provided or in a personal journal. Writing can bring clarity and deeper understanding of yourself and of God's Word.

5. It might be good to have a Bible dictionary handy. Use it to look up any unfamiliar words, names or places.

6. Use the prayer suggestion to guide you in thanking God for what you have learned and to pray about the applications that have come to mind.

7. You may want to go on to the suggestion under "Now or Later," or you may want to use that idea for your next study.

Suggestions for Members of a Group Study

1. Come to the study prepared. Follow the suggestions for individual study mentioned above. You will find that careful preparation will greatly enrich your time spent in group discussion.

2. Be willing to participate in the discussion. The leader of your group will not be lecturing. Instead, he or she will be encouraging the members of the group to discuss what they have learned. The leader will be asking the questions that are found in this guide.

3. Stick to the topic being discussed. Your answers should be based on the verses which are the focus of the discussion and not on outside authorities such as commentaries or speakers. These studies focus on a particular passage of Scripture. Only rarely should you refer to other portions of the Bible. This allows for everyone to participate in in-depth study on equal ground.

4. Be sensitive to the other members of the group. Listen attentively when they describe what they have learned. You may be surprised by their insights! Each question assumes a variety of answers. Many questions do not have "right" answers, particularly questions that aim at meaning or application. Instead the questions push us to explore the passage more thoroughly.

When possible, link what you say to the comments of others. Also, be affirming whenever you can. This will encourage some of the more hesitant members of the group to participate.

5. Be careful not to dominate the discussion. We are sometimes so eager to express our thoughts that we leave too little opportunity for others to respond. By all means participate! But allow others to also.

6. Expect God to teach you through the passage being discussed and through the other members of the group. Pray that you will have an enjoyable and profitable time together, but also that as a result of the study you will find ways that you can take action individually and/or as a group.

7. Remember that anything said in the group is considered confidential and should not be discussed outside the group unless specific permission is given to do so.

8. If you are the group leader, you will find additional suggestions at the back of the guide.

1

The Purpose of God

We have a love-hate relationship with God's will. We dearly want to discover it and obey it, to be secure in knowing we are following the path he desires. On the other hand, we definitely don't want to find out what he wants because deep down we suspect it may not be to our liking.

GROUP DISCUSSION. On a piece of paper complete the following statement. I feel God's will is: (a) a ball and chain around my neck, (b) a goal to reach, (c) reassuring, (d) unknowable, (e) something to rejoice in, (f) something to fear, (g) something to discover and then do, or (h) other: _____. Write down a brief explanation for your answer. Now, fold up the papers and have each person choose one. Read each response and try to guess who wrote it. Talk about why you think that response characterizes that person.

PERSONAL REFLECTION. Recall ways that God has revealed his will to you over the course of your life. What patterns do you see? Thank God for his guidance.

In this study we'll see what Paul says about God's will. *Read Ephesians 1:1-14.*

---

1. According to verses 3-6, what blessings are ours from the Father?

What other blessings, according to verses 7-12, do we have in Jesus Christ?

What blessings do we receive through the Holy Spirit (vv. 13-14)?

---

2. Which of these is most significant to you? Explain.

---

3. What strong words and phrases throughout the passage describe God's actions toward us? (For example, "chose" in v. 3.)

4. The notion of being "chosen" and "predestined" is strong here. What is Paul's emotional reaction to being chosen and predestined?

What is yours?

5. From the information given in 1:1-14 alone, try to formulate a clear statement of what it means to be chosen by God.

6. According to verses 9-10, God has blessed us by revealing that the ultimate goal of history is to bring all things under Christ. What does this mean?

7. Summarize God's redeeming purpose from eternity past to eternity future as described in 1:3-14.

8. What do you discover in these verses about God's attitude toward us (note especially vv. 5, 9)?

9. What does it mean to live "to the praise of his glory" (vv. 6, 12, 14)?

How can we do this?

10. How has this passage increased your sense of participation in God's total purpose for the universe? Explain.

Spend time in praise to the God and Father of our Lord Jesus Christ, who has blessed us with every spiritual blessing.

Now or Later

Go back through the passage again noting what God has done, is doing and will do for you. Be sure to note God's attitude toward you in all that he is doing. Write a letter of thanks to God.

2

"I Keep Asking"

Ephesians 1:15-23

Sometimes prayer can be as difficult as pushing a full wheelbarrow—with no wheel. At other times the flow of prayer takes over—like rushing down the rapids of a mountain river. It can be especially difficult to pray for those we are deeply concerned about when we are confused about their needs and what might be best for them. It can also feel very natural to pray for those we love as we bring them before God and express our love.

GROUP DISCUSSION. Today's study is about the things we ask God to do for one another. Before you get serious about prayer, have some fun talking about three wishes. If a genie were to pop out of a bottle, what would you ask for?

PERSONAL REFLECTION. Talk to God about times prayer for others has been hard for you. Perhaps you feel guilty about being inconsistent in your commitment to pray for someone. Describe your disappointment or pain. Take time to allow him to listen to you fully.

Paul's prayers for the Ephesians overflowed with praise and thanksgiving. *Read Ephesians 1:15-23.*

1. How do Paul's prayers for his readers cover the past, the present and the future?

2. In verses 15-16 Paul says, "For this reason . . . I have not stopped giving thanks for you, remembering you in my prayers." Why is Paul so thankful in his prayers for the Ephesians?

3. Describe the qualities that Paul's prayers for the Ephesians focus on.

Why do you think he focuses his prayer in this way?

4. What can you learn about praying for others from Paul's prayers?

5. What experiences of the power described in verse 18 have you had?

6. According to verses 22-23, how is the church, the body of believers, central to God's plans for the universe?

7. What role does the church play in your life?

8. How do verses 20-23 expand on Paul's discussion of Christ's head-ship that began in verses 9-10?

9. What is the connection between the content of verses 1-14 and the prayers of verses 15-23?

What can you learn from this for your own prayer life?

Pray for Christ's church and individuals in your church, following Paul's example.

Now or Later

We can learn a great deal about praying for others from Paul's letters. *Read 2 Thessalonians 1:1-12.* What do you learn about praying for others from these verses?

If someone were to pray for you as Paul did in verses 11-12, what is one specific way you would want God to change your life?

3

Amazing Grace

Ephesians 2:1-10

One of the best-known verses in the book of Ephesians is 2:8: "By grace you have been saved, through faith." Grace has often been defined by the acrostic God's Riches At Christ's Expense.

GROUP DISCUSSION. How might your life be different if God ceased to be gracious to you?

PERSONAL REFLECTION. Focus on God's graciousness to you in the past days, weeks and months. Allow yourself to experience the depth of his goodness. Respond to him in prayer and praise.

In this study we'll consider some of the riches we have been given in Christ. *Read Ephesians 2:1-10.*

1. According to this passage, what are the effects of being dead in transgressions and sins?

2. How have you seen sin kill?

3. According to verses 4-7, what motivated God to save us?

4. How do you respond to these motives as you consider our condition without Christ?

5. Glance back at 1:19-20. What parallels do you see between 1:19-20 and 2:4-6?

6. What does Paul mean when he says we have been "made alive," "raised" and "seated" with Christ (vv. 5-6)?

7. How does our union with Christ relate to the fulfillment of God's purpose stated in 2:7?

8. What difference does the reality of your union in Christ make in your everyday life?

9. What do we learn about God's grace from 2:8-10?

_____

10. When Paul says that our salvation is not from ourselves (vv. 8-9), is he saying that we play no role in our salvation? Explain.

_____

11. Does verse 10 contradict verses 8-9? Explain.

_____

12. What good works has God prepared for you to do?

_____

13. What has hindered you from doing these?

Thank God specifically for some of the many ways he has been gracious to you. Ask him to remove the barriers to the good works he has created for you to do.

Now or Later

Reflect on how or when it is difficult for you to be a recipient of God's grace. Journal on each of the areas that come to mind. Comment on why you think receiving God's grace might be difficult for you.

Talk to God about what you have journaled.

4

We Are One

Many of us have sung, "We are one in the Spirit; we are one in the Lord." But we also continue to find ourselves at odds with Christians who believe or live differently than we do. Such problems were just as common in Paul's day as in ours.

GROUP DISCUSSION. Find as many things as possible that you all have in common.

PERSONAL REFLECTION. Take time to feel and reflect upon the negative feelings that you have toward certain individuals or groups. In a journal describe the situation, your feelings and the reason for these feelings as honestly as you can. Commit each situation to God in prayer. Ask him to open your mind and your heart so that you can develop understanding about yourself and him as well as the situation and that you would be changed by him.

Paul longed for the Gentile Christians to know how they had been brought near to God through the blood of Christ and were one with their Jewish brothers and sisters. *Read Ephesians 2:11-22.*

1. Paul uses vivid imagery in this passage. What are some of these images?

What are they intended to communicate?

2. Verse 11 emphasizes the distinction between those who are circumcised and those who are uncircumcised—the Jews and the Gentiles. What name-calling do Christians engage in today—perhaps even using biblical terms?

3. Besides some superficial differences between Jews and Gentiles, there were also some very real divisions. What are some of the things that divided Gentiles from Jews (v. 12)?

4. How does the bond we have in the blood (death) of Christ supersede all that divides us from other Christians (v. 13)?

5. According to 2:14-18, what two reconciliations does Christ achieve?

6. How have you found that being reconciled to God through Christ affects your being reconciled to others?

7. Paul says Christ destroyed the dividing wall "by abolishing in his flesh the law with its commandments and regulations" (v. 15). In what sense did the cross abolish the law?

8. What rules, written or otherwise, and requirements do we enforce which might hinder people from coming into the kingdom?

9. We still see divisions among Christians today even though Christ himself is our peace (vv. 14-18). How can those who are united in Christ still be divided?

10. How do the images Paul uses in 2:19-22 emphasize the unity Christians have with one another?

11. How is the reconciliation of Jews and Gentiles to each other and to God (2:11-22) one fulfillment of God's will and purpose in Christ (1:9-10)?

12. How can you learn more about the views of others so that you can work toward unity?

13. What practical first step toward unity can you take in the next week with Christians you differ with?

Commit to God those relationships in your life where you need to be reconciled to other Christians. Ask God to break down the walls that separate you from your brothers and sisters.

Now or Later

Think about one broken relationship in your life. Ask God for compassion for and understanding of that person. Make a plan for the steps that you will take to attempt to make the relationship right.

5

Prisoner &
Preacher

Ephesians 3

What do you think of when you hear the word *church*? A building on the corner? A stuffy group of religious hypocrites? A vibrant fellowship?

GROUP DISCUSSION. When have you had a particularly powerful experience in the church?

PERSONAL REFLECTION. Think of two or three adjectives which summarize your attitude and experience of the church. Reflect on what has made church difficult and what has made it special. Pray for your church and thank God for it.

Paul's special ministry enables him to enlarge our conception of the church. In this passage Paul clarifies and exalts the place of the church in God's plan. *Read Ephesians 3.*

---

1. What themes do you see throughout this chapter?

2. Paul says that he has been a recipient of God's grace in two ways. God revealed to him a mystery, and he was given the privilege of preaching to the Gentiles the riches of Christ. Explain the meaning of the mystery revealed to Paul (vv. 2-6).

3. What purpose does God have for the church (vv. 10-11)?

4. How does your attitude toward the church compare and contrast with Paul's?

5. How does this purpose for the church mesh with God's overall purpose in Christ described in 1:9-10?

6. Paul was in prison "for the sake of you Gentiles" (v. 1). How then was Paul's imprisonment to the glory of his readers (3:13)?

7. Paul now turns from instruction to prayer. Three times in verses 14-21 Paul mentions "love" and "power." What do we learn about power and love in these verses?

8. In what specific ways do you see God's love and power in your life and in the life of your church?

9. Verses 10-11 state that the church is to make known God's wisdom. How is Paul's prayer directed toward fulfilling that purpose?

10. How is God's wisdom being made known through your local body of believers?

11. To what extent has his prayer been answered in your life or in the life of your church?

12. In what specific ways are you encouraged and motivated by the benediction in verses 20-21?

Using Paul's prayer as a guide, pray for yourself and your church.

Now or Later

In your journal describe what it would look like to have each of the requests in Paul's prayer answered in your life and church.

6

Unity &
Uniqueness

While Ephesians 1—3 provides a doctrinal foundation, Ephesians 4—6 shows in practical detail how to give glory to God in the church. Paul now considers the quality of life that is demanded of believers individually and in the fellowship of Christ's church.

GROUP DISCUSSION. "To have unity we must all be uniform." Explain why you do or do not agree with this statement.

PERSONAL REFLECTION. Ephesians 4:2 says, "Be completely humble and gentle; be patient, bearing with one another in love." Reflect on these words. Measure your recent behavior against them. Talk to God about what you discover.

Paul is so concerned for these Christians that he *begs* them to lead a life worthy of their calling.

1. According to Ephesians 1—3, what is our calling?

2. *Read Ephesians 4:1-16.* What are the characteristics of a life which is worthy of our calling (vv. 1-3)?

3. Why are these virtues so important for maintaining unity?

4. Which qualities help you foster unity with others, and which do you still need to work on?

5. We are commanded to keep the unity of the Spirit. But Paul also says we already have one body, one Spirit, one hope, one Lord, one faith, one baptism and one God and Father of all. How do these seven "ones" contribute to actually living out true unity?

6. In verses 8-10 Christ is compared to a conquering hero whose triumphal procession fills "the whole universe," from the highest heaven to the lowest earth. He then generously distributes gifts (the spoils of victory) to his loyal followers. What is the nature and purpose of these gifts (vv. 11-13)?

7. What spiritual gifts do you think you might have?

8. How do they fulfill the purposes described in 4:11-13?

9. How does spiritual infancy differ from spiritual maturity (vv. 14-16)?

10. What winds and waves are blowing and tossing the church today?

11. While 4:16 sets forth the unity we have as believers, 4:7-11 describes our uniqueness through the individual gifts we have received. How does Paul's explanation of the proper function and goal of these gifts bring us right back to the opening theme of Ephesians 4?

---

12. In verse 16 Paul says that the body "grows and builds itself up in love, as each part does its work." What steps do you need to take to more fully work toward this goal?

Pray that your spiritual gifts will be used to help others grow in Christ and to build the church.

Now or Later

Even as our spiritual gifts are used for building up the body of Christ, so members of the body of Christ help us identify what our gifts are. Meet with a Christian friend or two who know you well and consider together what spiritual gifts you may each possess.

7

Something Old, Something New

Already and not yet. That's how we experience Christ. Already we have come out of spiritual darkness and into his light. Already we have received his grace and come to know him. But not yet do we live completely the way God wants. We have not yet arrived. Still, Jesus is right beside us on this journey.

GROUP DISCUSSION. Do Christians necessarily live better lives than non-Christians? Explain.

PERSONAL REFLECTION. When have you felt that you were lost in darkness? What brought you into the light? Spend time praising God for his redemption.

Paul continues to flesh out what it means for his readers to live a life worthy of their calling (4:1). *Read Ephesians 4:17-32.*

1. How does Paul contrast the life of the Gentile (unbeliever) with that of a true believer throughout these verses?

---

2. Paul says the Gentiles are afflicted with a spiritual condition known as hardness of heart (v. 18). What are the effects of this condition (vv. 17-19)?

---

3. What steps in our lives might indicate movement toward a hard heart?

---

4. What do you think it means to put off the old self (v. 22)?

---

5. How do your attitudes affect the way you live (v. 23)?

---

6. In verses 25-32 what does Paul tell us to put off, what does he say to put on, and what reason does he give for doing these things? (If he doesn't explicitly state each of the three parts for a given topic, fill in what is implied.)

Put Off   **Put On**   **Reason**

7. How do these instructions show the importance of healthy communication in promoting unity?

---

8. Which of the commands in verses 25-32 do you have difficulty following? Explain.

---

9. What practical steps could you take this week to improve your relationships with others in an area of difficulty?

---

10. Which of the commands in verses 25-32 have you seen God strengthen you to obey?

Spend time praising God for his work in your life, and pray that he will give you grace in the areas needing improvement.

Now or Later

Take some time to journal on some of what you have learned from this passage. Consider again what we are to put off and put on according to verses 25-32. Write out both negative and positive examples of these from your life. Use them as a guide for prayer.

8

Live in Love, Live in Light

Ephesians 5:1-20

We are always grateful to find out that our kids haven't taken part when their friends are ridiculing someone. However, we are thrilled when they defend the person being teased and let their friends know that humiliating a person is unacceptable.

Not doing what is wrong is one thing. But sometimes it can be even more difficult to do what is right.

GROUP DISCUSSION. How do children imitate? (Give some examples from your own observations of small children.)

PERSONAL REFLECTION. Think about people you have or would like to imitate. What makes you want to imitate them?

In Ephesians 5 Paul continues to outline what it means "to live a life worthy of the calling you have received" (4:1). He does this by considering ways we shouldn't act and ways we should. Just as children imitate their parents, so we are to imitate God. *Read Ephesians 5:1-20.*

1. What would it be like to imitate God in some way?

2. According to verse 2 Christ is the perfect example of imitating God by living a life of love. What difference does it make to you that Christ has gone before you in living this life of love?

3. What behaviors does Paul condemn (vv. 3-4)?

4. How is thanksgiving an appropriate replacement for the behavior Paul condemns in verses 3-4?

5. How can you use thanksgiving to replace improper behavior in your life?

6. Why will immoral, impure or greedy people be unable to inherit the kingdom (vv. 5-7)?

7. Why are such people considered idolaters?

8. In verses 8-14 Paul contrasts light and darkness to say more about holy living. According to these verses, what does it mean to "live as children of light"?

9. In what ways do you struggle with living as a child of light?

10. Often we equate wisdom with intelligence. What characterizes wise people according to verses 15-17?

11. How can you live more wisely then?

---

12. In your own words, explain the characteristics of those who are filled with the Spirit (vv. 18-20).

---

13. According to Paul's definition of filling, in what area do you most need to be filled with the Spirit?

Talk to God as a child to a father. Tell him how you would like to imitate him.

Now or Later

Spend some time singing and making music in your heart to the Lord with "psalms and hymns and spiritual songs" (5:19). Write a psalm of your own expressing to God your gratitude to him for the life he has called you to live.

9

Love & Respect

Ephesians 5:21-33

A lot of emotion and misunderstanding surround the word *submit*. So try to come to this text as if you had never seen it before. Try to set aside your own biases and see what Paul really has to say on the subject of submission.

GROUP DISCUSSION. How do you react to the idea of being told to submit to someone?

PERSONAL REFLECTION. How has God shown you that he is faithful and trustworthy? Express your thanksgiving for his care.

In this passage Paul considers how the relationship between Christ and the church can be a model for wives and husbands. *Read Ephesians 5:21-33.*

1. How does verse 21 set the tone for this entire passage?

2. How is your willingness to submit to others affected by your reverence for Christ?

3. Paul says wives are to submit to their husbands as to the Lord (v. 22). What does it mean to submit to the Lord?

---

4. Why is the church's submission to the Lord a helpful illustration of a wife's submission to her husband?

---

5. If you are a wife, how could your submission to your husband grow more like your submission to Christ? (Or if you are single, how can you grow in your submission to Christ?)

---

6. Does submission mean putting your mind in neutral? Explain.

---

7. In verse 25 Paul instructs husbands to love their wives as Christ loved the church. How has Christ shown his love for the church?

---

8. The word *love* in 5:25 and 28 is used to translate the Greek word *agapaō*, meaning "totally unselfish, sacrificial love." How are husbands to show love for their wives (vv. 25-30)?

9. If you are a husband, how could your love for your wife grow more like Christ's love for the church?

---

10. In verse 31 Paul quotes Genesis 2:24 to root his arguments about the unity of husband and wife in creation itself. How do verses 31-33 summarize his teaching on the unity that is to exist between wives and husbands?

---

11. Why do you think Paul calls on wives to respect their husbands while he calls on husbands to love their wives (v. 33)?

---

12. How can you show more love and respect to others?

Tell Christ in prayer how you would like to more fully submit your life to him. If you are married, talk to God about the ways he wants to change the ways you respond to your spouse.

Now or Later

Paraphrase the verses which describe how Christ loves the church and all that he has done for her. Reread your paraphrase and respond to God, telling him what this means to you.

10

Honor & Obey

Ephesians 6:1-9

How much our parents mean to us—yet they can be difficult! How much we love our children—yet they are exasperating at times!

GROUP DISCUSSION. How would you characterize the relationship you have had with your parents?

PERSONAL REFLECTION. Reflect on the finest qualities of your parents (or of parenting in general). Consider which of these you have experienced in your relationship with God. Take time to thank him.

In nine packed verses Paul not only delves into the important relationships between parents and children but those of the work world as well. *Read Ephesians 6:1-9.*

1. How does this passage continue the theme of mutual submission that began in 5:21?

2. What reasons are given for obeying and honoring parents (vv. 1-3)?

3. In your own life (or in the lives of others), how have you seen the promise given to those who honor their parents fulfilled?

4. Is it possible to obey parents without honoring them? Explain.

5. What are some practical ways you can obey or honor your parents?

6. How can fathers (and mothers) exasperate their children (v. 4)?

7. Why does Paul contrast exasperating children with bringing "them up in the training and instruction of the Lord" (v. 4)?

8. If you are a parent, what can you do this week to follow verse 4 more closely? (If you are not a parent, how have you seen verse 4 in action?)

---

9. What is implied about the way slaves normally worked for their masters (vv. 5-8)?

---

10. How and why were Christian slaves to be different?

---

11. How could the principles Paul outlines in verses 5-8 be lived out in situations you have been in or are in?

---

12. Paul says masters should treat slaves the way he wants slaves to treat masters because both have the same Master in heaven. Why should this make a difference in how slaves are treated?

13. What implications does this have for how employers treat employees?

---

14. How does this passage contribute to the theme of the church glorifying God through visible unity?

Pray that in all you do you would serve "wholeheartedly, as if you were serving the Lord."

Now or Later

Write a letter to your parents expressing your thanks to them for all that they have been to you and have done for you. If your parents are not alive, write that letter to God.

Write a letter to your parents expressing all that you forgive them for. Write this even if they are not alive. Do not send the letter but use it in prayer as you ask God for the ability to forgive and for healing where you have been wounded by your parents.

11

Prayer Wars

In a war of bullets, careful aim and heavy armor win battles. In a war of words, eloquent speech and sharp pens overcome the opposition. But if the fight is outside the realm of sight, sound and touch, how are victories won?

GROUP DISCUSSION. How do you respond to the idea that there are spiritual forces in the universe that are working against God's will?

PERSONAL REFLECTION. How have you recently seen God protecting you as you face spiritual battles?

In this study we will look at how the ultimate battle is fought and how it can be won. *Read Ephesians 6:10-24.*

1. In 6:10-12 Paul emphasizes that our struggle is not with flesh and blood. How has he emphasized this same point elsewhere in his letter?

2. How do you sense a battle around you with more than physical forces and foes?

3. Four times in verses 11-14 Paul urges his readers to stand firm in the battle against the devil. How are we susceptible to instability as Christians?

4. When Paul wrote Ephesians, he may have been chained to a Roman soldier (v. 20). This could easily have inspired his analogy of 6:13-17. How does the "armor of God" prepare us for spiritual battle?

5. Which piece of armor do you need most to fight your spiritual battles? Explain.

6. In 6:10-12 Paul identifies our ally and enemies in battle. In 6:13-17 he considers our preparation and tactics. Now, according to verses 18-20, how is the battle itself fought? Explain your answer.

7. In 6:18-20 Paul urges all kinds of prayers. How has he been a model of a prayer warrior throughout this letter?

8. What main obstacle do you face in fighting the battle of prayer more effectively?

9. What step might you take to stand firmly against your spiritual opponents?

10. How has your awareness of spiritual realms been expanded through this letter?

11. Throughout this study of the book of Ephesians we have referred to 1:9-10 often. How has your vision of God's plan and purpose for the universe been expanded?

Take time now to pray about your fight in spiritual warfare.

Now or Later

Participating in war is not fun. What fears do you have as you think about what it means to face spiritual warfare? What doubts do you entertain about the reality of spiritual battle and unseen enemies? Talk to God about the battle and thank him for the victory through Jesus Christ our Lord.

Leader's Notes

Leading a Bible discussion can be an enjoyable and rewarding experience. But it can also be *scary*—especially if you've never done it before. If this is your feeling, you're in good company. When God asked Moses to lead the Israelites out of Egypt, he replied, "O Lord, please send someone else to do it"! (Ex 4:13). It was the same with Solomon, Jeremiah and Timothy, but God helped these people in spite of their weaknesses, and he will help you as well.

You don't need to be an expert on the Bible or a trained teacher to lead a Bible discussion. The idea behind these inductive studies is that the leader guides group members to discover for themselves what the Bible has to say. This method of learning will allow group members to remember much more of what is said than a lecture would.

These studies are designed to be led easily. As a matter of fact, the flow of questions through the passage from observation to interpretation to application is so natural that you may feel that the studies lead themselves. This study guide is also flexible. You can use it with a variety of groups—student, professional, neighborhood or church groups. Each study takes forty-five to sixty minutes in a group setting.

There are some important facts to know about group dynamics and encouraging discussion. The suggestions listed below should enable you to effectively and enjoyably fulfill your role as leader.

Preparing for the Study

1. Ask God to help you understand and apply the passage in your own life. Unless this happens, you will not be prepared to lead others. Pray too for the various members of the group. Ask God to open your hearts to the message of his Word and motivate you to action.

2. Read the introduction to the entire guide to get an overview of the entire book and the issues which will be explored.

3. As you begin each study, read and reread the assigned Bible passage to familiarize yourself with it.

4. This study guide is based on the New International Version of the Bible. It will help you and the group if you use this translation as the basis for your study and discussion.

5. Carefully work through each question in the study. Spend time in meditation and reflection as you consider how to respond.

6. Write your thoughts and responses in the space provided in the study guide. This will help you to express your understanding of the passage clearly.

7. It might help to have a Bible dictionary handy. Use it to look up any unfamiliar words, names or places. (For additional help on how to study a passage, see chapter five of *How to Lead a LifeBuilder Study*, IVP, 2018.)

8. Consider how you can apply the Scripture to your life. Remember that the group will follow your lead in responding to the studies. They will not go any deeper than you do.

9. Once you have finished your own study of the passage, familiarize yourself with the leader's notes for the study you are leading. These are designed to help you in several ways. First, they tell you the purpose the study guide author had in mind when writing the study. Take time to think through how the study questions work together to accomplish that purpose. Second, the notes provide you with additional background information or suggestions on group dynamics for various questions. This information can be useful when people have difficulty understanding or answering a question. Third, the leader's notes can alert you to potential problems you may encounter during the study.

10. If you wish to remind yourself of anything mentioned in the leader's notes, make a note to yourself below that question in the study.

Leading the Study

1. Begin the study on time. Open with prayer, asking God to help the group to understand and apply the passage.

2. Be sure that everyone in your group has a study guide. Encourage the group to prepare beforehand for each discussion by reading the introduction to the guide and by working through the questions in the study.

3. At the beginning of your first time together, explain that these studies are meant to be discussions, not lectures. Encourage the members of the group to participate. However, do not put pressure on those who may be hesitant to speak during the first few sessions. You may want to suggest the following guidelines to your group.

☐ Stick to the topic being discussed.

☐ Your responses should be based on the verses which are the focus of the discussion and not on outside authorities such as commentaries or speakers.

☐ These studies focus on a particular passage of Scripture. Only rarely should you refer to other portions of the Bible. This allows for everyone to participate in in-depth study on equal ground.

☐ Anything said in the group is considered confidential and will not be discussed outside the group unless specific permission is given to do so.

☐ We will listen attentively to each other and provide time for each person present to talk.

☐ We will pray for each other.

4. Have a group member read the introduction at the beginning of the discussion.

5. Every session begins with a group discussion question. The question or activity is meant to be used before the passage is read. The question introduces the theme of the study and encourages group members to begin to open up. Encourage as many members as possible to participate, and be ready to get the discussion going with your own response.

This section is designed to reveal where our thoughts or feelings need to be transformed by Scripture. That is why it is especially important not to read the passage before the discussion question is asked. The passage will tend to color the honest reactions people would otherwise give because they are, of course, supposed to think the way the Bible does.

You may want to supplement the group discussion question with an icebreaker to help people to get comfortable. See the community section of the *Small Group Starter Kit* (IVP, 1995) for more ideas.

You also might want to use the personal reflection question with your group. Either allow a time of silence for people to respond individually or discuss it together.

6. Have a group member (or members if the passage is long) read aloud the passage to be studied. Then give people several minutes to read the passage again silently so that they can take it all in.

7. Question 1 will generally be an overview question designed to briefly survey the passage. Encourage the group to look at the whole passage, but try to avoid getting sidetracked by questions or issues that will be addressed later in the study.

8. As you ask the questions, keep in mind that they are designed to be used just as they are written. You may simply read them aloud. Or you may prefer to express them in your own words.

There may be times when it is appropriate to deviate from the study guide. For example, a question may have already been answered. If so, move on to the next question. Or someone may raise an important question not covered in the guide. Take time to discuss it, but try to keep the group from going off on tangents.

9. Avoid answering your own questions. If necessary, repeat or re-phrase them until they are clearly understood. Or point out something you read in the leader's notes to clarify the context or meaning. An eager group quickly becomes passive and silent if they think the leader will do most of the talking.

10. Don't be afraid of silence. People may need time to think about the question before formulating their answers.

11. Don't be content with just one answer. Ask, "What do the rest of you think?" or "Anything else?" until several people have given answers to the question.

12. Acknowledge all contributions. Try to be affirming whenever possible. Never reject an answer. If it is clearly off-base, ask, "Which verse led you to that conclusion?" or again, "What do the rest of you think?"

13. Don't expect every answer to be addressed to you, even though this will probably happen at first. As group members become more at ease, they will begin to truly interact with each other. This is one sign of healthy discussion.

14. Don't be afraid of controversy. It can be very stimulating. If you don't resolve an issue completely, don't be frustrated. Move on and keep it in mind for later. A subsequent study may solve the problem.

15. Periodically summarize what the group has said about the passage. This helps to draw together the various ideas mentioned and gives continuity to the study. But don't preach.

16. At the end of the Bible discussion you may want to allow group members a time of quiet to work on an idea under "Now or Later." Then discuss what you experienced. Or you may want to encourage group members to work on these ideas between meetings. Give an opportunity during the session for people to talk about what they are learning.

17. Conclude your time together with conversational prayer, adapting the prayer suggestion at the end of the study to your group. Ask for God's help in following through on the commitments you've made.

18. End on time.

Many more suggestions and helps are found in *How to Lead a LifeBuilder Study*.

Components of Small Groups

A healthy small group should do more than study the Bible. There are four components to consider as you structure your time together.

Nurture. Small groups help us to grow in our knowledge and love of God. Bible study is the key to making this happen and is the foundation of your small group.

Community. Small groups are a great place to develop deep friendships with other Christians. Allow time for informal interaction before and after each study. Plan activities and games that will help you get to know each other. Spend time having fun together—going on a picnic or cooking dinner together.

Worship and prayer. Your study will be enhanced by spending time praising God together in prayer or song. Pray for each other's needs—and keep track of how God is answering prayer in your group. Ask God to help you to apply what you are learning in your study.

Outreach. Reaching out to others can be a practical way of applying what you are learning, and it will keep your group from becoming self-focused. Host a series of evangelistic discussions for your friends or neighbors. Clean up the yard of an elderly friend. Serve at a soup kitchen together, or spend a day working in the community.

Many more suggestions and helps in each of these areas are found in the *Small Group Starter Kit*. You will also find information on building a small group. Reading through the starter kit will be worth your time.

Study 1. Ephesians 1:1-14. The Purpose of God.

Purpose: To consider God's plan and purpose for all of history and all of creation, and the blessings he has given us as part of that plan.

Group discussion. For groups only. Be sure to have a set of small sheets of paper (which look all the same) ready. If necessary, let group members know that the intent is to get to know one another better—not to see if you can disguise your identity. Group members should be honest about their doubts and questions, but not flippant.

Personal reflection. These ideas are designed for individuals who want to have a more meditative or devotional experience. If you are leading a group, you could also allow a time of silence for members to pray in this way as they come into God's presence.

Question 1. This is an observation question asking for specific privileges and benefits that belong to us in Christ.

Question 3. Notice words and phrases like "the will of God," "chose," "predestined," "according to the plan" and "the purpose of his will."

Question 4. While praise is not merely emotional, it seems clear from the vigor of this passage that Paul has a very profound emotional response. This could be an important emphasis for people who tend to intellectualize their faith or equate it with a mere series of propositional truths.

Question 5. Try not to let the discussion deteriorate into a bull session on predestination versus free will. Rather, focus on what the passage says. What does it mean to be chosen? For example, Ephesians says that predestination affects our status in Christ. It does not say that every facet of our every action is controlled and foreordained by God.

Verses 11-14 also show that predestination does not necessarily limit the scope or availability of salvation. "In him we [the Jews] were also chosen. And you [the Gentiles] also were included in Christ."

Adoption was a Roman custom (not a Jewish one) which emphasizes that our status is solely due to the will of the adopter and not to any right we have inherited by birth. Very early in his letter Paul indicates the equality of Jews and Gentiles in the kingdom.

Question 6. Verse 10 should not be mistaken as supporting universalism—the belief that all will be saved. Rather, it teaches that Christ will reign over all of creation.

Question 8. God does this "in accordance with his pleasure"! Notice also rich words like *lavished* (v. 8).

Question 9. The glory of God is evident when God is revealed or made known. To live to the praise of his glory is thus to live and worship God in words and deeds. It is also to lead others to know him better and to praise him. Thus worship and evangelism are linked very closely, as are worship and study.

Study 2. Ephesians 1:15-23. "I Keep Asking."
Purpose: To view the model of prayer Paul offers us as he intercedes for the church.

Group discussion. Of course God is not a genie who magically does our bidding. Rather the point of the question is to help people get in touch with their deep longings. Here's another opening question you can use before you begin: "When you pray for other Christians, how do you usually pray for them? Give some specific examples."

Question 1. The past can be seen in verses 15 and 20. The present in verses 16-17 and 21-23. The future in verses 18-21.

Question 3. Note that Paul focuses on wisdom, revelation and knowledge. (But don't get hung up on the differences among them.) Notice also the rich language of verse 18. Discuss why he chooses these particular qualities.

Question 6. Some scholars have felt that 1:23 indicates that the church makes Christ complete. But the reverse is the more natural interpretation and is more consistent with the rest of the letter (see 4:9-16). Christ makes the church a complete expression of his power, position and person. The church is central to Christ's headship over all creation.

Question 8. From time to time questions will link together passages previously studied. You may need to take time to review this material, especially if everyone was not present. It is important to note how the themes are tied together to gain perspective on the book as a whole.

Question 9. Verses 1-14 contain a prayer of thanksgiving and verses 15-23 is a prayer of intercession which flows naturally out of praise.

Study 3. Ephesians 2:1-10. Amazing Grace.
Purpose: To see how God has brought us from death to life by the riches
of his grace.

Question 2. This question is meant to put flesh on the words in verses 1-3.
You might need to take a phrase such as "gratifying the cravings of our sinful
nature and following its desires and thoughts" and ask what evidence of this
the group has seen in their own lives or in the world and what the damaging
effects have been. Modeling honesty in application of Scripture is one of the
best ways to have group members respond honestly.

Question 3. Help the group to look carefully at God's motivation. There
is marvelous truth in this passage that we may think that we understand.
The things we do understand we have a tendency to take for granted.

Question 5. Help the group to observe in both passages what happened
to Christ and what happened to Christians.

Question 6. Ephesians 2:5-6 refers to Christ being "made alive," "raised"
and "seated." The Apostles' Creed formulated it this way: "The third day
he rose again. He ascended into heaven, and is seated at the right hand of
the Father." But what is so remarkable in Ephesians is that Paul is not
just writing about Christ but about us as well. We now share a union
with Christ who rules in the heavenly places.

By now the group should be starting to catch on that Ephesians 1:9-10
is the nub of the whole letter. God is bringing everything in the universe
under Christ, and out of his love and mercy he has graciously chosen to
begin with us, his people, as a sign of the complete fulfillment of his purpose which is yet to come.

Question 10. We receive "the gift of God" through faith. Thus we are
actively involved as God saves us.

Question 11. This is not an easy question. Can good works be an important and necessary part of our lives without being the basis for our salvation? Allow discussion to flow freely, but bring the group's attention back
to the passage as needed.

Questions 12-13. If the group will thoughtfully interact with these questions it can lead to an exciting and meaningful discussion. It is a way to
think about how we are a part of God's purpose being fulfilled. So often
we think of our lives as being unimportant. Sometimes it is difficult for
people to talk about the good works they know they are involved in

because it can sound like bragging. But they are God's good works and he has prepared us to do them. We are simply recognizing what he is doing and the glory is his.

Study 4. Ephesians 2:11-22. We Are One.

Purpose: To see that Christ's death not only reconciled us to God but also to each other, and to consider the implications of this.

Question 1. The whole letter is incredibly rich in imagery and metaphorical language. In this passage especially, Paul can hardly get an idea out without using some kind of analogy to geographic distance, physical structures, new people, peace treaties and the like. If you want the group to understand Paul, you have to understand his imagery.

Question 2. According to the *New Bible Commentary:*

> The first section calls the predominantly Gentile-Christian readers to remember their former status as those outside God's people. They were then what many Jews would call "the uncircumcision." Circumcision was the seal of the covenant with Israel, and so what distinguished Jews from the rest of the world. Judaism could thus refer to itself as *the circumcision*, meaning "the covenant people of God," and dismiss the rest of the world, who stood outside the covenant, as "the uncircumcision." The point was not that Jews alone practiced the minor surgical operation (other Semites did too), but its significance as a rite of entry into the Mosaic covenant.
>
> Paul begins his description of the Gentiles' former position using the language any Jew might to point to their "outside" status. It is equally clear, however, that Paul is not actually happy with this way of putting things, and feels he needs to qualify it by clarifying that Jews are only *those who call themselves "the circumcision."* For Paul, theirs is a circumcision merely performed by men, because, for him, their circumcision is often no more than an external surgical act, and the relationship to God it is supposed to symbolize has not become an internal reality worked by God. For Paul it is the household of *faith* whose relationship to God actually fulfills what circumcision is about (see Rom. 2:28-29), and this is most deeply true of Christians (Phil. 3:3; Col. 2:11). (G. J. Wenham et al., eds. [Downers Grove, Ill.: InterVarsity Press, 1994], p. 1230)

Encourage the group to think about Christians they disagree with over doctrine or practice—even if it is a "friendly" disagreement. We create categories like charismatic versus noncharismatic and Reformed versus dispensational. Or perhaps white versus black, Catholic versus Protestant, Moral Majority versus Christian pacifists will be among the conflicts mentioned. There might be others as well that are closer to the concerns of your group. There are many ways that Christians engage in name calling today.

Another way of looking at this or asking the question is: "What kind of boxes do we place other Christians in?" Sometimes we say disparagingly that someone does "such or such" or believes "such and such" when they haven't even discussed it with that person to find out what they really do or believe. **Question 3.** Richard Foulkes writes:

> The Jews were named the people of God. The Gentiles were not. The Jews were the Circumcision or the people whose men had on them the mark of the covenant of God. The Gentiles were called the Uncircumcision. The Gentiles were without Christ and without the hope of the Messiah. They were cut off from the fellowship and privileges of those who called themselves the people of God. They stood almost entirely outside the spiritual privileges of Israel. Finally, Paul says that they were without God. The Greek word here (*atheoi*) does not mean that they refused to believe in God, or that they were forsaken by God, or godless in their conduct, but they had no real knowledge of God. Some sought for the One in philosophy; some tried to come within the fold of Judaism. But by and large the Gentiles had to live in the world lives limited by the things of the world, and had to face the trials and sorrows and perplexities of the world without the knowledge of God to interpret the whole. (*The Epistle of Paul to the Ephesians,* Tyndale New Testament Commentaries [Grand Rapids, Mich.: Eerdmans, 1956], pp. 78-80)

Question 4. According to the *New Bible Commentary:*

> Now, *in Christ* (13), their situation has dramatically changed, and Paul chooses a common biblical metaphor to express the contrast. The imagery of the *near* and *the far away* originated in Is. 57:19, and it dominates Paul's description as far as vs 17-18 (where he actually uses the Isaiah wording). In v. 13, however, he uses the language in a way that more closely reflects a special use of it in contemporary Judaism. The verb "to make near" had become a term for making a non-Jew a proselyte, and so joining him or her to the congregation of Israel. This made the person concerned "near" in two senses, both of which are attested in Judaism. He or she becomes "close" to the rest of the people of God and "close" to the God to whom the

people are "near." They have access to the temple (the special place of divine presence) and to the God who was more generally present amongst his people. As we shall see, Paul is thinking of a transformed people of God and a heavenly temple, but otherwise his imagery in v 13 is similar. (p. 1231)

This truth of course relates not only to Jewish and Gentile Christians but all Christians today. We are not to be divided from other Christians. The death of Christ has brought us near to God and near to each other, the people of God.

Question 7. There was a literal "dividing wall of hostility" (2:14) in Jerusalem. The Court of the Gentiles was separated from the Temple proper by a stone wall. This wall had a sign on it forbidding entrance to any foreigner on pain of death.

Question 8. The issue, of course, is, what is the essential gospel? What minimal requirements, if any, are there before we can say someone is in fellowship with us? Are we guilty of creating artificial barriers to God like some Jewish Christians who required gentile Christians to be circumcised? Ask the group to be honest. Almost all of us have some notions of what it means to be a "real" Christian based on extrabiblical requirements.

Study 5. Ephesians 3. Prisoner & Preacher.
Purpose: To look at the purpose of the church and its role in fulfilling God's plan.
Question 2. According to the *Dictionary of Biblical Imagery:*

Ephesians lets its readers in on a cosmic secret, a "mystery," a chapter of God's eschatological plan that was laid "before the foundation of the world" (1:4), that was formerly concealed and now has been revealed n Christ. This mystery has been made known to Paul by a revelation (Eph 3:3)— though it has also been revealed to other apostles and prophets by the Spirit (Eph 3:5)—and the opening two chapters of Ephesians unfolded Paul's understanding of the mystery (Eph 3:4). The essential outline of the mystery is that Gentiles are now fellow heirs, members of the same body, sharers in the promise with believing Israelites who have followed Jesus Christ (Eph. 3:6). But the mystery includes a vertical dimension, the union of Christ with his church, a "great mystery" (Eph 5:32). The mystery has not been revealed to the cosmic powers but the curtain is now being lifted and the mystery disclosed to them. The "rulers and authorities" are spectators as the wisdom of the Creator God's cosmic drama is now being acted out in the story of the church." (Leland Ryken, James C. Wilhoit and Tremper Longman III, eds.[Downers Grove, Ill.: InterVarsity Press, 1998], pp. 240-41)

Question 5. Throughout the book of Ephesians, we will continue to see different aspects of God's overall purpose for the world. At times we will turn our attention back to Ephesians 1:9-10 where this purpose of God is so clearly stated.

Question 6. The Jews who arrested him reacted against the kind of teaching Paul has just expressed in Ephesians 2. Namely, Jesus has abolished the divisive elements of the law and is creating a new people and building a new temple.

Question 9. A pun is at work in the original Greek in 3:14-15 since "Father" is *pater* and "family" is *patria*. So Paul could mean, "I kneel before the father, the source of fatherhood." It could also again emphasize the oneness of lineage both Jews and Gentiles have together, that being of "Abraham's seed" is not nearly so crucial as being a child of God.

Study 6. Ephesians 4:1-16. Unity & Uniqueness.
Purpose: To see the place of unity and of unique gifts in the body of Christ.

Question 5. In *The Message of Ephesians* John Stott writes: "To maintain the church's unity must mean to maintain it visibly. Here is an apostolic exhortation to us to preserve in actual concrete relationships of love . . . that unity which God has created and which neither man nor demon can destroy" ([Downers Grove, Ill.: InterVarsity Press, 1979], p. 152).

Question 6. The explanation is included before this question is asked in order to avoid confusion about a very obscure passage. If members still have questions, ask if they could be discussed after the study. For now, focus on what we can draw out from these verses—Christ can and does give his people unique gifts.

Question 7. According to the *New Bible Dictionary,* in the New Testament there are nine Greek words for "gift." Some of them refer to our gifts to God, some our gifts to one another. A key word is *charmisa:* "Its characteristic use is for the 'spiritual gifts', *i.e.* the gifts which the Holy Spirit imparts to certain people. Everyone has such a gift (1 Pet. 4:10), but specific gifts are reserved for individuals (1 Cor. 12:30), and individuals endowed with these gifts are themselves 'gifts' to the church (Eph. 4:7ff.).

The important passages are Rom. 12:6ff.; 1 Cor. 12:4-11, 28-30; 14; Eph. 4:11ff" (p. 411).

Because Peter states that "each one should use the gift that he has received to serve others" (1 Pet 4:10), it is certainly worthwhile to ask the Holy Spirit to reveal to you what your gifts are. Friends in your Christian community could give you feedback on what they have observed in you. Understanding what your spiritual gifts are and how God is using them in the church and in the world will contribute to your life of ministry.

None of the lists of gifts in the New Testament passages are complete. Various classifications of the gifts have been attempted, but they fall most simply into two main categories—those which qualify their possessors for the ministry of the Word such as apostles, prophets and teachers, and those which equip them for practical service such as administration, hospitality and generosity.

Certainly other gifts besides those in Ephesians 4 could be mentioned. But in general be careful that your whole discussion is not taken up on this point. How do you know you have these gifts? How can you develop them? And so on.

If your group has no background in thinking about spiritual gifts you need not spend a great deal of time on them now. You might share a few of the above thoughts and give them the references to study. You might want to follow up on this topic at another meeting designated for that purpose.
Question 10. If pressed for time, this could be skipped.

Study 7. Ephesians 4:17-32. Something Old, Something New.
Purpose: To consider the purity of conduct and communication necessary for maintaining unity in the body of Christ.
Question 2. The passage essentially has two halves. Questions 2-6 cover verses 17-24. Questions 7-12 cover verses 25-32.
Question 3. This is an application question that could be difficult to answer for a couple reasons. First, it is not easy to admit to others that we have experienced "hardness of heart" even if we know that we have. Second, we may not know that our hearts are hardening if they are. Hardness of heart, as we see in this passage, does not happen overnight. It is a slow, subtle process. It begins when we allow thoughts that do not honor God or which separate us from God to stay in our minds. Next we lose sensitivity to the things of God

and the way that he wants us to live. Then comes the giving over of ourselves to sensuality and impurity—"with a continual lust for more."

It is possible to have moments or stages of hardness of heart toward God but moving out of it. Or it is possible to continue in the process which finally ends with our giving ourselves over to sensual and impure living. Paul insists that Christians must not live this way. So it is important for the follower of Jesus to be alert to the beginning steps which lead to hardness of heart and that they resist going that way and thus helpful to discuss our own experience with hardness of heart.

Question 4. The command to put off our old self (our life before Christ) when we have already been made new in Christ is parallel to the command to maintain unity when we are already one (4:34). We are to visibly act on the spiritual reality of being new creatures in Christ by discarding our old ways of life.

Putting off the old self is choosing to no longer live as the Gentiles do, in the futility of their *thinking* (v. 17). It is to put off the old way of thinking and to think differently—the way God wants you to think. It is in the attitude of our minds that we are made new. Romans 12:2 says, "be transformed by the renewing of your mind." It is contrasting our folly with God's wisdom.

Question 6. Don't get hung up on filling in the outline in detail or hassling about exactly which piece goes where. In fact, if each person did their own list, probably none of the lists would look alike. The purpose of the question is to give people a handle on what could otherwise look like a string of disconnected instructions. It is important to grapple with the behaviors that Paul has instructed them to put on and take off. Considering the reasons behind his instructions can strengthen the motivation to do what he says.

Study 8. Ephesians 5:1-20. Live in Love, Live in Light.

Purpose: To continue to examine what it means for us to live worthy of our calling.

Questions 6-7. Some confusion could arise in your group over verses 5-6. These verses may seem to imply that we are saved by works apart from faith. In 5:3-4 Paul is speaking of individual acts which should be avoided. In verse 5 he switches from individual acts to the whole person, condemning a complete way of life, an entire orientation away from God's will. He spoke of such people previously in 2:1-3 and 4:17-19. The "immoral, impure or greedy person" is not condemned for isolated sinful acts but for his or her lifestyle.

Why would Paul raise such an issue if he is addressing Christians primarily? He was probably combating the proto-Gnostic belief quite prevalent then that sins were irrelevant to one's spiritual state. No doubt many of his readers were influenced by such thinking. So he emphasizes, "Let no one deceive you." Obviously, an idolater is one whose life is not ruled by God but by some other passion. By definition, then, one whose lifestyle is idolatrous is cut off from God and subject to his wrath. There will be no need to go into this issue, of course, if it does not come up or your group is not troubled by it.

Question 10. Don't be distracted by preconceived ideas of what it means to be "filled with the Spirit." Focus the group's attention on what Paul says it means.

Now or Later. Bring hymnbooks or song sheets with you to the study for the group to use. Or sing songs you all know by heart. If you have a guitarist in the group or a piano at hand, use these. If your group isn't made up of singers, then do as Paul suggests and "speak to one another with psalms, hymns and spiritual songs."

Study 9. Ephesians 5:21-33. Love & Respect.

Purpose: To consider how the relationship between Christ and the church can be a model for wives and husbands.

General note. Hang onto your hats; there's a good chance this will be your most controversial study. But don't be afraid of controversy itself or of strong differences of opinion. Try to present an atmosphere of openness and willingness to hear all sides. However, don't hesitate to ask people to root their contentions in the passage. Your purpose is to see what Paul says here and not to bring in a myriad of outside resources and opinions. Before you start, you may want to remind everyone to stick to the passage!

Question 1. Paul's instructions for both husbands and wives are given in the context of mutual submission (5:21), though Paul sees this acted out in different ways. Submission in either case, however, is counting others better than yourself. Paul calls on both husbands and wives to do this—

husbands especially submitting to their wives by loving them and sacrificing whatever is necessary to meet their needs; wives especially submitting to their husbands by respecting them and honoring them as their head (see questions 11-12).

Question 2. Although this study is about the marriage relationship, there are applications to our relationship with Christ (questions 2 and 5) and to anyone in the body of Christ (v. 12). Be sensitive to singles in your group and try to help them feel included in the study.

Questions 5, 9. We suggest that you make it clear to the group when a question is addressed to women and when it is addressed to men. Do not allow one gender to speak for or to evaluate the other. This is consistent with the fact that Paul addresses husbands and wives separately.

Note that verses 22-24 are instructions to *wives* in how they are to conduct themselves in marriage. They are not instructions to husbands on how they are to make their wives behave or on what they have a right to expect as husbands. Likewise verses 25-30 are instructions to *husbands* in how they are to conduct themselves in marriage. They are not instructions to wives on how they are to make their husbands behave or on what they have a right to expect as wives. Paul emphasizes the responsibilities of each and makes no comment on the rights of either. Thus we hope that in questions 5 and 9 men do not respond when women are addressed or vice versa. The intent is for both to consider for themselves what their responsibilities are and how to respond.

Question 11. In verse 33 Paul summarizes the different responsibilities of each spouse. Perhaps the reason for the difference is that while all human beings need both love and respect, women tend to feel more need for love, and men tend to feel more need for respect. Likewise it is often easier for women to give love and for men to give respect. So Paul focuses on the tougher assignment for each and on giving what the other needs most.

Question 12. If you are leading a group in which all participants are married, this last question could be: If you are a woman, how could you show respect to your husband? If you are a man, how could you show love to your wife?

Study 10. Ephesians 6:1-9. Honor & Obey.
Purpose: To discover how Paul's discussion of parents and children and

masters and slaves contributes to his theme of glorifying God through our unity.

Group discussion. If people have trouble getting started, you could suggest one word answers: Stormy? Loving? Nonexistent? Casual? Close? Stiff? Open? Allow a few minutes for all to speak who wish to.

Question 1. This study opens with a question giving an overview of the whole passage and closes with a question that reviews it (question 14). Don't get into a lot of detail here since that is coming later. Look for general comments and observations.

Question 2. Some commentators see the promise of verse 3 as general rather than particular, applying to a family or family line or society as a whole rather than to an individual.

Question 3. Some group members may find this and other questions in this passage difficult to answer depending on what their relationship with their parents is or was like. Try to be aware of how people are feeling.

Question 4. Be ready for and open to negative answers. If they come, don't try to preach your position. Allow the group to struggle with the issues.

Question 5. If question 4 generates controversy, question 5 could bring things back together. Encourage the group to be concrete in how they will obey and honor their parents, if only in small ways.

Question 8. If there are parents in your group, be sure you don't just cover the second half of verse 4 but the first half as well.

John Stott writes, "The instruction to children to obey their parents presupposes . . . parental authority. Yet when Paul outlines how parents should behave towards their children, it is not the exercise, but the restraint, of their authority which he urges upon them" (*Message of Ephesians*, p. 245).

In the New Testament era slavery was not the violent system that was found in the United States. It was more like being an indentured servant, and with that role there was a great deal of freedom.

> Outside Palestine . . . where the churches were often established on a household basis, the membership included both master and servants. Slavery was one of the human divisions that became meaningless in the new community in Christ (1 Cor. 7:22; Gal. 3:28). This apparently led to a desire for emancipation (1 Cor 7:20) and perhaps even to the active encouragement of it by some (1 Tim. 6:3-5). Paul was not opposed to manumission if the opportunity was

offered (1 Cor. 7:21), but studiously refrained from putting pressure on owners, even where personal sentiment might have led him to do so (Phm. 8, 14). Not only was there the practical reason of not laying the churches open to criticism (1 Tim. 6:1f.) but the point of principle that all human stations are allotted by God (1 Cor. 7:20). Slaves should therefore aim to please God by their service (Eph. 6:5-8; Col. 3:22). The fraternal bond with a believing master should be an added reason for serving him well (1 Tim. 6:2). A master, on the other hand, might well let the fraternal sentiment prevail (Phm. 16), and certainly must treat his slaves with restraint (Eph. 6:9) and strict equity (Col. 4:1). The fact that household slavery, which is the only kind referred to in the NT, was generally governed by feelings of goodwill and affection, is implied by its figurative use in the "household of God" (Eph. 2:19). (I. Howard Marshall et al., eds., *The New Bible Dictionary* [Downers Grove, Ill.: Inter-Varsity Press, 1996], pp. 1113-14.)

Study 11. Ephesians 6:10-24. Prayer Wars.

Purpose: To grasp how the ultimate battle is fought and how it can be won.

Group discussion. There may be some in your group who do not believe in a personal devil. Allow them to express their views without getting into a big discussion of whether or not they are right. As the study moves on, Paul's position should become plain.

Question 2. See for example 1:3, 21; 2:2, 6; 3:10. (This question and question 7 ask you to look over the whole book of Ephesians. This can help tie the book together while touching on various points in 6:10-24.)

Question 4. Ephesians 3:1 and 4:1 also indicate his imprisonment.

Don't feel obligated to cover every piece of armor. It's more important to get the general idea of how we are prepared.

Question 7. If the group has trouble with this, first help them to look closely at 6:18-20, and describe Paul's prayer life from his comments about prayer and his prayer requests. How does he demonstrate a dependence on prayer? Then look back through the book to evidence of his being a prayer warrior. In 1:3 and following we see Paul full of praise to God and naming specific reasons for this praise. Examine Paul's prayers in 1:15-23 and in 3:14-20. How might we model our praying after Paul?

Andrew T. Le Peau is the former editorial director of InterVarsity Press, where he worked for over forty years. Phyllis J. Le Peau is an area director for InterVarsity Christian Fellowship in the Chicago metro area. They are also the authors of the LifeBuilder Bible Study James.